Prosperity

And

Success

Generate, Attract and Recieve

I0150124

Ranvir

Alight Publications

2008

Prosperity And Success
by Ranvir

First Edition Published in July 2008

Alight Publications
PO Box 930
Union City, CA 94587

http://www.Alightbooks.com

ISBN 1-931833-30-3

Printed in the United States of America

For my wife

CONTENTS

Introduction

Everyone is seeking happiness in life, whether they are willing to admit or not. Very few are willing to make the effort to secure this happiness they desire.

Some seek happiness in wealth and possessions. Others seek it in wisdom and higher consciousness. Still others, in a balanced, stable, stress-free life with meaningful relationships.

Many who have acquired immense wealth have not achieved happiness - they were bereft of the wisdom to utilize their resources and merely wasted them to satisfy fleeting desires. All their relationships were tarnished by distrust. How many real-life soap-operas have we observed in the break-ups of wealthy families?

It is true that happiness is not dependent on external sources and that a person who achieves the liberation of Self-Realization is constantly connected to the source of bliss and joy. However, for those treading the spiritual path, it can be long and frustrating - there is no guarantee of success without great effort and the grace of the Divine. Indeed, there can be great suffering and misery for those struggling on the path. Is this suffering necessary or can there be a smoother way? It is possible for monks and/or renunciates to retire to their reclusive monasteries and caves, but what about those spiritual householders who have duties and responsibilities? They need to feed, clothe and house their families.

Prosperity is the combination of wealth, wisdom, health, family, friends and overall well-being - happiness.

The Laws of Prosperity and Success

There is a misunderstanding that one can just sit around and call upon the Divine to help us. Just as there are physical laws, there are spiritual laws laid down by the Divine -- we are all familiar with the Law of Karma. There are many more laws that govern the the subtle realms.

In the stories that follow, the laws that govern prosperity and success are explained -- please do take some time to understand them.

Do not be confused by the experience that wealth and success seem to come to those who are strong and ruthless -- sooner or later, suffering and failure will be their lot.

There are 4 methods given for generating prosperity and success:
1. The recitation of power hymns called **stotras**
2. The practice of **mantras** or sacred power vibrations
3. The simple ritual of **puja**
4. The commitment to an annual **Vrat**

These methods are explained in the appropriate sections.

The keys that ensure the retention of prosperity are:
A. The **effort** of performing the techniques **generate** the energy for prosperity and success.
B. It is **wisdom and dispassion** which **attract** the generated energy of prosperity and success.
C. The virtues of **honesty, integrity, love and compassion** sustain the **continous receipt** of prosperity and success.

The Source of Prosperity

In Ancient India, there was a rich and powerful king who was never satisfied with his lands and wealth. He was especially jealous of his cousins, whom he'd plotted against many times. The eldest cousin was an upright and noble king, who always managed to re-gain his prosperity, despite all the subterfuges.

The jealous king went to his aged and blind father to learn from him the explanation on how the noble king always came out on top. The father instructed his son by telling him the following story:

There were incessant wars between the forces of light, led by the hero-god Indra and the forces of darkness led by various demon kings. At one time, the demon king was Prahlada, who had transformed his nature to such an extent that he was able to annex the domains of the gods and men by the force of his character and made himself Lord of the three worlds.

Dispossessed, but undaunted, Indra went to the high priest of the gods, Brihaspati, and with all humility, begged him to teach him the means by which he could re-gain his spiritual leadership. Brihaspati taught him the means and said that if he practiced steadfastly it would lead him eventually to paramount virtue.

Indra then asked how that path leading him to spiritual and moral character could be shortened, and Brihaspati counseled him to go learn from the teacher of all the demons. However when the king of light approached the teacher of all the demons, he was in turn counseled to learn directly from his nemesis Prahlada.

Putting on the guise of a spiritual seeker, Indra approached Prahlada and begged him to teach him the path to prosperity. However Prahlada was fully occupied with the administration all the three worlds and told the disguised Indra that he had no time to take a student. In response Indra fell down at the feet of Prahlada and pleaded that he would wait as long as necessary for instruction from such supreme preceptor.

Pleased with such earnestness, Prahlada chose an auspicious hour to begin, proceeded to teach the highest wisdom to his student, the hero-god. After receiving the teaching in reverence and humility, Indra inquired of Prahlada how he had obtained lordship of the three worlds.

Prahlada replied, "I am never proud that I am king; I do not treat the learned and holy ones with derision. Listening to their words of wisdom I discipline myself and give liberally. They speak to me in confidence and I let myself be guided by them in all things. The sages establish me safely and securely in *dharma* as the bees confine honey in the honeycomb. I have conquered anger and my senses are under my control. In this way I live in the company of those whose speech keeps pace with their understanding, delighting in the light of knowledge. The words of wisdom coming from the lips of a learned person – that is the basis of all prosperity."

After some time had passed, pleased with his student's service and attention, Prahlada offered him a boon and asked him to request whatever he wanted. Whereupon Indra said, "if you are pleased with me and would give me anything I ask for, I would ask for the gift of your character. Please give me your moral character."

Naturally, Prahlada was taken aback by this request and was quite beside himself for a while. Yet a promise is a promise and a boon granted could not be revoked by a noble person. He therefore regretfully made a gift of his entire moral character to the disguised Indra who immediately thanked him and left.

Prahlada was sitting and thinking about what had happened when a spirit of great luster emanated from his body and in response to his startled question said, "I am your moral character and you have divested yourself of me and so I'm going to reside in your student." It then disappeared into the body of Indra.

No sooner had this spirit disappeared, and another great light arose from Prahlada and said, "I am *dharma* and I'm going to your student because I can only reside where there is moral character. Then a third spirit came out of Prahlada's body, even brighter than the previous two and declared himself to be the spirit of truth or *satya* who goes where *dharma* goes.

Immediately after the departure of *satya*, the spirit of good conduct *vritta* rose up together with the spirit of strength, and both left, because strength and good conduct are inseparable.

To make matters worse, a lustrous woman of great divinity appeared and prepared to leave. Prahlada tried to stop her, but she responded, "I am Lakshmi - everything that makes for whatever it is auspicious and for prosperity, and I must follow the strength and valor which has left you."

Prahlada realized how his pride and rashness had deprived him of his high moral character. This humbled him and he completely surrendered himself to the Absolute Divine, from whom he had received everything, and to whom he had been so devoted in his childhood. He gave up all desires for the material world and achieved liberation.

So this is how the Lord of the gods, Indra recovered lordship of the three worlds, by learning the secret of moral character from Prahlada. This secret is, "in thought, word and deed, one should refrain from harming any creature. Compassion and giving are the marks of good character. One should not do what may injure another or whatever one would feel ashamed of. Do only that which evokes approval in the assembly of sages. This is the sum and essence of moral character. Even though some people may appear to be prosperous in the world who are not strong in moral character, their prosperity will not last long for its roots are neither deep nor strong. Therefore acquire the virtue of moral character if you wish to attain to lasting prosperity."

Unfortunately, the jealous king did not listen to his father and left unsatisfied. Soon after, he forced a great war against his cousins, but even though he had much larger forces, he was totally destroyed by the upright king.

Key #1
Prosperity and Success are dependent on strength and valor, which in turn are dependent on truth and right action, which in turn are dependent on virtue.

Churning the Cosmic Ocean

Once Indra, the king of gods, came across a sage named Druvasa who offered him a sacred garland. Indra was riding on an elephant and so carelessly put the garland, a symbol of success, on the trunk of the elephant. The elephant was irritated by the smell and threw it on the ground. The enraged sage cursed Indra and all the devas or gods to be bereft of fortune, strength and energy, as the garland was a dwelling of Sri or Lakshmi.

The devas (gods) and asuras (semi-divine beings) were constantly at war in the whole of the cosmos. Following this incident, the devas were defeated and the asuras gained control of the universe. The asuras desired the nectar of immortality but could not obtain it without the help of the defeated gods.

The churning of the Ocean of milk, was an elaborate process. Mount Meru was used as churning rod and Vasuki, the King of Serpents, became the churning rope. The gods held the tail of the snake while the asuras held the head end of the snake and they pulled on it alternately causing the mountain to rotate which in turn churned the ocean. However, once the mountain was placed on the ocean, it began to sink but Akupara, the king of tortoises came to their rescue and supported the mountain on his shell back.

The churn twisted and turned, the ocean frothed and fumed, waves roared and spewed foam in every direction. Eons passed. Nothing emerged. But the gods and demons continued to churn the great ocean.

Pleased by their efforts, the goddess finally emerged as Lakshmi the desirable one, in all her splendor.

.

Seated on a dew drenched Lotus, dressed in red silk, bedecked in gold, she was the very embodiment of affluence, abundance and auspiciousness.

As she rose, *rasa*, life giving sap, began flowing in every direction. The gods saluted her; the asuras sang songs to her glory.

Key #2

Effort is needed to obtain Prosperity and Success.

One cannot sit around and expect the universe to do all for us. We must act properly at the right time. Success comes to those who have prepared for it.

The Rise and Fall of Bali

The *devas*, gods, admired the beauty of Lakshmi while the *asuras* or semi-divine beings, craved her wealth. They fought many a battle over who should possess her. Finally, under the leadership of Bali, the *asuras* emerged triumphant.

Impressed by Bali's strength, the goddess Lakshmi came to him as Shreedevi and crowned him king of the earth, for she was also Bhoodevi or the Goddess of Earth. She offered him a throne, a footstool and held a parasol over his head.

Shreedevi's sacred white elephants turned into clouds and sprinkled life-bestowing rain upon the earth, watering fields and pastures so that crops grew abundantly and cows gave plenty of milk. Everyone was happy with Bali as their king.

Power made Bali arrogant. He declared, "The earth belongs to me; I can give anyone anything he desires." He took over rulership of heaven as well because the devas had no power to oppose him.

Indra, leader of the *devas*, meanwhile, bereft of Shreedevi's grace had been reduced to poverty. He approached the Lord Vishnu and asked for his help. The Lord told Indra to be patient and that he had a plan and will help them when the time came.

As time went by, Bali's pride and arrogance knew no bounds and he began to treat Shreedevi as his right and possession which disturbed the goddess and she began to withdraw from hiim.

In due time, Indra was told by Vishnu to approach Bali and supplicate the king for some land. To mock him, Bali pointed to Vamana the dwarf and said, "I shall give you as much land as this little one can cover in three strides."

Unfortunately for Bali, Vamana was no ordinary dwarf but rather an incarnation of Vishnu. As soon as Bali said this, Vishnu began to grow in size, turning into a giant who strode across and claimed all of Bali's kingdom in two steps. With his third step Vishnu shoved Bali into the nether region.

Vishnu thus wrested control of the earth for the gods and Indra was restored to his throne in heaven.

Key #3

Strength & Power initially attract Success

Pride and arrogance chase away Success

Wealth and Power Corrupt

Indra Disappoints

After Indra returned to heaven, he beseeched Lakshmi to stay there.

"The gods may lack strength, but they are intelligent. I shall go to them." So saying, Shreedevi went to the gods. She blessed the gods with ruling majesty, material prosperity, physical health, bodily beauty and divine fortune.

Angry and bitter in defeat, the asuras complained, "Shreedevi is **Chanchala**, the fickle one. Once she favored Bali, now she favors Indra. She is faithful to none."

"That is not true," said the goddess, "I am eternally faithful to he who does not abuse my gifts."

The goddess continued, "He who takes good care of the earth-goddess Bhoodevi, wins the affection of Shreedevi, goddess of fortune and becomes king of the cosmos."

But Indra did not heed her words. Soon after being crowned king, the leader of the *devas,* he retired to the pleasure gardens. There, he drank wine, enjoyed song and dance and neglected his royal duties.

The earth, left ungoverned was plundered.Bhoodevi's lamentation fell on deaf ears. This made Shreedevi very angry. She turned away from Indra.

Key #4

Pleasure and Comfort Corrupt

Dharma or Duty is necessary for the grace of Prosperity

Birth of Misfortune

Along with Lakshmi rose Alakshmi, the goddess of barrenness and misfortune from the churning of the cosmic ocean. She was ugly with matted hair, sunken cheeks, shriveled breasts and coarse limbs.

Said the goddess, "Lakshmi will dwell where there is nobility and righteousness, cleanliness and beauty, virtue and compassion. Alakshmi will dwell elsewhere, attracted by sloth, envy greed, lust and pride."

Key #5

Purity of body and mind keep misfortune away

Birth of Earth and Abundance

In the beginning, chaos and order battled for supremacy and there was nothing to eat and nowhere to live. Primeval water was everywhere. Prajapati, the divine patriarch, father of the gods and asuras saw the plight of his children and invoked the Primeval Mother.

The Mother informed him that under the water was the Earth (Bhoodevi) and that if she was raised up, then there would be food and shelter for their children.

Prajapati took the form of a mighty boar called Emusha, plunged into the sea and found the earth-goddess Bhoodevi on the ocean floor. Placing her on his snout, he gently raised her to the surface.

Prajapati then turned into Akupara, a giant turtle and offered Bhoodevi a seat on his back.

Seated on the celestial turtle, the earth-goddess nurtured life in her bountiful arms. She offered food and shelter to all.

Key #6

Sacrifice and Compassion give birth to Abundance

The Gifts of Bounty

With Lakshmi came a cow called Kamadhenu with enough milk to feed the world for all eternity, a wish fulfilling gem called Chantamani and a tree called Kalpataru that bore every flower and fruit desirable. In her hand she held the basket of bounty: the Akshaya Patra overflowing with grain and gold.

There also appeared Kama the delightful god of pleasure. Riding his parrot surrounded by bees and butterflies, this handsome god raised his sugarcane bow and shot arrows dripping with desire into the heart of every being. He roused the senses, excited the mind and inspired the heart.

With Kama came Priti and Rati, goddess of love and longing and Vasantathe lord of the spring. Wherever they went flowers bloomed bees buzzed to welcome them with offerings of nectar and pollen.

Behind Lakshmi stood Rambha, the beautiful nymph who knows sixty-four ways to pleasure the senses and Sura, the goddess of intoxicants who can soothe tired nerves and enchant the mind with dreams.

Gods and asuras became enamoured by these gifts and fought mightily to acquire and keep them. Lakshmi herself was forgotten and laughingly, she left them.

Key #7

Pursuit of desires and pleasures chase away prosperity and success

---

Marriage of Lakshmi

The goddess had also brought forth a throne, a crown, a footstool, a parasol, a fly-whisk, a cushion, a fan, a bow and a conch. "These symbols of kingship," she said, "will go to a worthy being - one who will use power to preserve and protect life."

Lakshmi sought someone who would not succumb to the allure of power, pleasure and prosperity; someone strong, wise and virtuous, capable of using force and skillful means with discretion to uphold the laws of life.

She asked Vishnu who had defeated Bali why he had let Indra become the king of heaven. "Don't you want to be lord of the universe and enjoy the splendors of the cosmos?" asked Shreedevi.

"I desire nothing. By defeating the demon Bali, I have done my duty. I seek no reward for it."

These words of Vishnu pleased Shreedevi and she placed Vaijayanati, the fragrant garland of victory round Vishnu's neck. He made her his consort and became known as Shreenatha, beloved of fortune.

Vishnu continues to battle the forces of chaos and corruption and diligently performs his duties as guardian of the world. Lakshmi accompanies him with her love and affection, tending to his every need as his devoted wife.

Key #8

Prosperity stays with Dispassion, Compassion and Duty

The Forms of Lakshmi

The images of Laskhmi are the favorite of most Indian homes and businesses. She is draped in a red saree, bedecked with gold ornaments, seated on a lotus, pot in hand, and flanked by white elephants.

Lakshmi, also called Laxmi, is the goddess of wealth, fortune, power, luxury, beauty, fertility, and auspiciousness. She holds the promise of material fulfillment and contentment. She has her arms raised to bless and to grant her blessings.

Shri is the sacred name of Lakshmi. Shri is written atop most documents and spoken before addressing a god, teacher, holy man or any revered individual. The word evokes grace, affluence, abundance, auspiciousness and authority. When the word is spoken or written, an aura of holiness is established. Whatever follows is imbued with divine blessing. Just as the word "Om" is associated with the mystical side of life, Shri is associated with the material side of existence.

Lakshmi represents the beautiful and bountiful aspects of nature. As Bhoodevi, the earth-goddess, she nurtures life; as Shreedevi, the goddess of fortune, she bestows power, pleasure and prosperity on those who deserve her grace. To realize her, one must respect the laws of life and appreciate the wonders of existence.

Lakshmi is also represented by a mystical diagram or yantra. One can use a photograph, a statue or a yantra to invoke her blessings.

Om Mahalakshmi Yantra

The word "Lakshmi" is derived from the Sanskrit word Laksme, meaning "goal." Lakshmi, therefore, represents the goal of life, which includes worldly as well as spiritual prosperity. Goddess Lakshmi, also called Shri, is the divine spouse of Lord Vishnu and provides him with wealth for the maintenance and preservation of creation.

In her images and pictures, Lakshmi is depicted in a female form with four arms and four hands. She wears red clothes with a golden lining and is standing on a lotus. She has golden coins and lotuses in her hands. Two elephants (some pictures show four) are shown next to the Goddess.

Her symbolism conveys the following spiritual themes:

The four arms represent the four directions in space and symbolize omnipresence and omnipotence of the Goddess. The red color symbolizes activity. The golden lining (embroidery) on Her red dress signifies prosperity - the Goddess is always busy distributing wealth and prosperity to the devotees.

The lotus seat, which Lakshmi is standing upon, signifies that while living in this world, one should enjoy its wealth, but not become obsessed with it. The lotus grows in muddy waters but stays pure and pristine above it.

The four hands represent the four ends of human life: *dharma* (righteous duty), *kama* (pleasures), *artha* (wealth), and *moksha* (liberation from birth and death). The front hands represent the activity in the physical world and the back hands indicate the spiritual activities that lead to spiritual perfection.

The right side of the body symbolizes activity - a lotus in the back right hand means that one must perform all duties in the world in accordance with *dharma*. This leads to *moksha* (liberation), which is symbolized by a lotus in the back left hand of Lakshmi. The golden coins falling on the ground from the front left hand of Lakshmi illustrate that she provides wealth and prosperity to her devotees. Her front right hand is shown bestowing blessings upon those who sincerely seek her help.

The two elephants standing next to the Goddess symbolize the name and fame associated with worldly wealth. The idea conveyed here is that you should not earn wealth merely to acquire name and fame or only to satisfy one's own material desires, but should share it with others in order to bring happiness to others in addition to oneself.

Some pictures show four elephants spraying water from golden vessels onto Goddess Lakshmi. The four elephants represent the four ends of human life as discussed previously. The spraying of water denotes activity while the golden vessels denote wisdom and purity. The four elephants spraying water from the golden vessels on the Goddess illustrate the theme that continuous self-effort, in accordance with one's *dharma* and governed by wisdom and purity, leads to both material and spiritual prosperity.

Goddess Lakshmi is regularly worshipped in home shrines and temples by her devotees. A special worship is offered to her annually on the auspicious day of Diwali, with religious rituals and colorful ceremonies specifically devoted to her.

The Eight Forms of Lakshmi

Lakshmi is commonly known as the Goddess of wealth. However, wealth is not only money, it is also tradition and values of life. Our family and progress are also wealth. Our belongings such as land, properties, animals, grains, etc as well as virtues like patience, persistence, purity etc in the form of character are nothing but our wealth and so also are glory or victory.

Mother Lakshmi is the source and provider of the following sixteen types of wealth and many more:
(1) Fame (2) Knowledge (3) Courage and Strength (4) Victory (5) Good Children (6) Valour (7) Gold and other gross properties (8) Grains in abundance (9) Happiness (10) Bliss (11) Intelligence (12) Beauty (13) Higher Aim, High Thinking and Higher Meditation (14) Morality and Ethics (15) Good Health (16) Long Life.

There is an eightfold functioning of Sri Lakshmi known as Sri Ashta Lakshmi -- each with individual nature and forms:

1. Adi Lakshmi: Mother Lakshmi resides with Lord Narayana (another name for Lord Vishnu) in Vaikuntha, the abode of Lord Narayana. She is known as Ramaa, which is bringing happiness to mankind. She is also known as Indira (who holds lotus or purity in the hands or heart.) This form of Divine Mother is seen serving Sri Narayana who represents omnipresence. Adi Lakshmi or Ramaa Lakshmi serving Sri Narayana is symbolic of her serving the whole of creation. Though Sri Narayana is attended by innumerable devotees, still she personally loves to serve the Lord. Actually mother Adi Lakshmi and Narayana are not two different entities but one only. We see her form sitting on the lap of Sri Narayana, as she represents his power.

2. Dhanya Lakshmi: Dhanya means grains. This includes all kinds of purified food containing all essential vitamins, minerals, protein, calcium, carbohytrade and so on. With the grace of mother Dhanya Lakshmi one gets all essential nutrients from grains, fruits, vegetables and other foods.

3. Dhairya Lakshmi: This form of mother Lakshmi grants the boon of infinite courage and strength. Those who are in tune with infinite inner power are always bound to have victory. Those who worship mother Dhairya Lakshmi, live and lead a life with tremendous patience and inner stability.

4. Gaja Lakshmi: The form of the elephant is very auspicious for wisdom and overcoming obstacles. The Sage Vyasa writes that Lakshmi came out of the ocean during the churning of the ocean (*Samudra Manthan*) - she is known as a daughter of the ocean. She came out of the ocean sitting on a full-bloomed lotus and also having lotus flowers in both hands. The two elephants by her sides, hold beautiful vessels filled with milk or nectar and are continuoulsy pouring it over Sri Lakshmi. During the festival of the lamps or the Deepavali, Ganapati or the Elephant God is also worshipped alongside with Mother Lakshmi - it signifies the protection from evils as well as abundant grace and blessings for additional prosperities!

5. Santan Lakshmi: In family life, children are the greatest treasure. Those who worship this particular form of Sri Lakshmi, known as Santan Lakshmi, are bestowed with the grace of mother Lakshmi and have wealth in the form of desirable children with good health and long life.

6. Vijay Lakshmi: Vijay is victory. Vijay is to get success in all undertakings and all different facets of life. Some people are strong physically but weak mentally while others are economically rich but poor in their attitude and cannot exert any influence. Vijay is to have all-encompassing victory. Vijay is to rejoice in the glory of our real nature – Vijay is to conquer our lower nature. Vijay is the victory in both external and internal wars! Those who invoke the grace of mother Vijay Lakshmi, have victory everywhere, at all times, in all conditions. Victory to Vijay Lakshmi !

7. Dhana Lakshmi: Dhana is wealth. According to the Purush Shukta of Rigveda, dhana is not only a wealth in coins and currency. Even the Sun and moon, fire and stars, rains and nature, oceans and mountains, rivers and streams, all these are our wealth, and so are our progeny, inner will power, character and virtues. With the grace of mother Dhana Lakshmi we will get all these in abundance.

8. Vidya Lakshmi: Vidya is knowledge and education. Education is not mere studies to receive the degrees, diplomas or certificates from the educational institutes or universities. Knowledge is not the accoumulation of useless data. Education which cannot give peace to the soul or cannot give the knowledge of the Self and inner satisfaction is not education. Education, which cannot wipe away the tears of others, known or unknown, is not education. Education is the understanding of the reality of every situation and the gracious art of living. It is living a life that lead to the Life Divine, where the ultimate goal is Self-Realisation.

True education can come only through discrimination and dispassion. One can have abundant amount of money, but if he does not know how to make good use of it, it will work to his disadvantage. If an alcoholic or a drug addict gets a huge sum of money, it will only hasten his downward journey to destruction. Vidya Lakshmi is the understanding and the knowledge to mold ordinary life into a spiritual life - a life of service, a life of compassion for fellow beings, a life of charity and generosity, a life of purity. It is a life for seeking the realisation of the absolute - the only real education, that can come only with the grace of Vidya Lakshmi.

Ultimately, all these eightfold forms of Sri Lakshmi are one single power only - that of Adishakti, the primordial universal power.

Adishakti is perennial and unchangeable, ever lasting, eternal truth or the absolute state of supreme blessedness. She is the origin. She is the light, the power, the wisdom and the strength. She is the supreme joy, peace, bliss and illumination.

May Mother Adishakti's and Sri Ashta Lakshmi's grace be ever upon all of us. May we receive her divine grace, that we may be fit as servants of mankind. May we realize the formless reality by the grace of these divine forms. Om shanti, peace!

Practices for generating the energy of prosperity

Since this is an Indian Tradition, the images and practices are all based on the realization of the sages who have formulated the universal laws in terms of mantras and yantras. By their application, the appropriate divine energy is generated.

The divine aspect of prosperity and success is known as Lakshmi and the techniques to attune to this divinity and generate the energy in one's life is given next. They do require the ability to learn the pronunciation of sanskrit words and to perform simple rituals.

It is important to remember that the generation of Lakshmi energy is not sufficient to ensure success -- one still needs to perform the actions that one would be doing anyway, with or without the blessings of Lakshmi. We cannot sit back and expect miracles without any effort from ourselves. She may bestow her blessings even if we have not performed any of these practices, but the probability of success is greatly inceased by the performance.

Practice #1

Stotras

Recitation of the mantric prayers to the Divine Mother of Prosperity and Success brings relief from distress and poverty. They bring success in both material and spiritual realms.

It is only necessary to choose one or two of the sacred power prayers given in the following pages, followed by the 108 names of Lakshmi. One can either learn them by memorisation or simply learn to read them aloud with ease.

The following stotras are given:

1. Shri Suktam
2. Ashta Laskshmi Stotram
3. Maha Lakshmi Ashtakam
4. Maha Lakshmi Stotram
5. Lakshmi Astotara Shantanam Stotram
6. Lakshmi Stuti

To invoke the blessings of Lakshmi, one should recite the chosen power prayers every Friday morning.

If one wishes to make greater progress, one can also repeat the chosen stotra every day at 6:30 pm, an auspicous time for the Divine Mother.

Sri Suktam

1

Hiranyavarnaam harineem
Suvarna rajatasrajaam,
Chandraam hiranmayeem
Jaatavedo mamaavaha.

O God of fire, please ask Lakshmi, the one who shines like gold, who destroys all sins, who is decked in silver and gold ornaments, whose face is like the full moon, and who is golden, to come here, and shower her grace on me.

2

Taam ma aavaha jaata vedo
Lakshmim anapagaaminim,
Yasyaam hiranyam vindeyam
Gaamashwam purushaanaham.

O God of fire, please ask that Sridevi, by whose grace, I got gold, cattle, and horses, as well as relatives and friends, to come here and shower her grace and stay with me always.

3

Ashwa poorva radha madhyaam
Hasti naadha prabhodhineem,
Shriyam devi upahvaye
Shrirmaa deveem jusataam.

I beseech and request that Sridevi whose procession is heralded by the trumpeting of elephants and full of horses and chariots, to come near me and shower her grace by being within me.

4

Kaam sosmitaam hiranya praakaram aardhraam
Jwalanteem truptaam tarpayanteem,
Padme sthitaam padma varnaam
Taam ehopahvaye shriyam.

I invoke and pray that the golden colored, ever shining and ever
smiling Mother who is the essence of happiness; who sits on the
lotus to be present here with me and shower me her mercy.

5

Chandraam prabhasaam yashaaa jwalantim
Shriyam loke deva jushtaam udaaraam,
Thaam padmineemeem saranamaham prapadhye Lakshmeerme
nasyatham twam vrune

I seek the protection of Mahalakshmi who is lustrous and shines
like the full moon. All of heaven worships her and her fame is all-
pervading. I take shelter at your lotus feet. Please destroy my
poverty forever.

6

Adhityavarne thamaso adhijaatho
Vanaspathisthva vrukshodha bilwa,
Tasya phalaani tapasa nudhanthu ma
Yaantharayascha bahya alakshmi.

O Universal Mother who shines like the sun, it is by your great
penance that the bilwa, holiest of trees was born.
It is the symbol of the tree of life. Let its fruits remove ignorance
within and without. Bless us with inner light and outer

7

Upaithu maam deva sakhaa keertheeya maninaa saha,
Pradhur bhoothosmo rashtresmin keerthim
vruddhim dadhathu me.

The god of wealth Kubhera, Who is the friend of Mahadeva,
Should come in search of me,
For I am born in this country, Showered with your grace,
Be pleased to give me fame and fulfillment.

8

Kshupthipaasa malaam jyeshtamalakshmim nasayamyaham,
Abhoothim masamrudheem cha sarva nirnudha me grahad.

I would remove Jyeshta*, Who creates hunger and thirst,
Wherever she lives, By your grace,
And please remove poverty and want from my house.

9

Gandhadwaaram dhuradapaa nithyapushtaam kareepineem,
Easwaree sarva bhoothaanam thaam ehopahvaye swayam.

I request and pray that Sridevi,
Who pleases others by sweet scent, Who cannot be defeated,
Who gives prosperity daily,
Who is full of everything, And who is the goddess of all beings,
To come and be present here.

10

Maanasa kamamaakrutheem vachassathya maseemahi,
Pasoonaam roopamannasya mayi sree srayathaam yasa.

I request goddess Sridevi, To forever bless me,
With fulfillment of good desires of the mind,
With ebbing happiness in life, With truth in my words,
And with beauty that plenty of food creates.

11

Kardhamena prajaa bhoothaa mayi sambhava kardhama,
Sriyam vaasaya me kule matharam padmamalineem.

O sage Kardhama** , In your house was born,
Goddess Sridevi as daughter, And so be pleased to be with me, So
that mother Lakshmi with lotus garland,
Is forever in my family, And bless us all with her grace.

12

Aapa srujanthu snigdhani Chikleetha vasa me gruhe,
Ni cha deveem matharam sriyam vasaya se kule.

O Sage Sikleedha***, Who is the son of Sridevi,
Let the goddess of water, Produce fatty products like milk and
ghee, And please come and live with us,
And request Goddess Sridevi, To live in our family forever.

13

Aardhraa pushkarineem pushteem suvarna hema malineem,
Sarvaa hiranmayeem lakshmim jathaveda ma avaha.

O god of fire, Be pleased to bless me,
So that Goddess Sridevi, Who is deeply merciful,
Who lives on a lotus, Who supplies food to the world,
Who is of golden colour, Who wears the garland of lotus,
Who makes us happy like the moon god, And who is purity
personified, To come and be with me.

14

Aardhraa ya karinim yashtim pingalaam padmalineem,
Chanraam hiranmayeem lakshmeem jathavedo ma avaaha.

O god of fire, Be pleased to bless me, So that Goddess Sridevi,
Who is deeply merciful, Who holds the staff of the emperor, Who
has a body like tender climbing plant,
Who has a pretty colour, Who wears golden garland,
Who shines like sun god, And who is purity personified,
To come and be with me.

15

Thaam ma avaha jathavedo Lakshmi managaamineem,
Yasyaam hiranyam prabhootham gaavo dasyoswaan vindheyam
purushapaanaham.

O god of fire, Be pleased to bless me, So that Goddess Sridevi, By
whose grace, I will get plenty of Gold,
plenty of cows, plenty of maidservants,
plenty of horses. And plenty of servants,
Never ever leave me.

16

Padmapriye, padmini, padmahasthe, padmalaye,
padmadalaayathakshi.
Viswapriye Vishnu manonukoole twat pada padmam mayi
sannidasthwa.

O Goddess Padmini, Who likes lotus flowers,
Who holds lotus flower in her hand, Who lives in lotus flower,
Who has broad eyes like the petal of lotus flower,
Who is the darling of the entire world, Who is dearest to Lord
Vishnu, Please keep your holy feet on me.

Maha devyai cha vidmahe, Vishnu patnai cha dheemahi,
Thanno Lakshmi prachodayath.

We will try to understand Mahadevi,
We would meditate on consort of Vishnu,
And let Goddess Lakshmi help us in this.

notes:
* Elder sister of Sridevi, the harbinger of bad luck and poverty.

** When Goddess Sridevi was born from the ocean of milk, she was brought
up by sage Kardhama

*** Some books mention him as the security guard of Sridevi and some others
equate him with God of love-manmatha.who is son of Sridevi.

Ashta Lakshmi Stotram

1. Adi Lakshmi [Primeval Lakshmi]:

Sumanasa vandhitha , madhavi
Chandra sahodhari hemamaye,
Munigana manditha , moksha pradhayini ,
manjula bhashini , veda nuthe,
Pankaja vasini deva supoojitha
sadguna varshani , santhiyuthe,
Jaya jaya hey madhusoodhana kamini
Adhilakshmi sada palaya maam.

Victory and victory to Adhi lakshmi
Oh, darling of the killer of Madhu,
Who is worshipped by all good people,
Who is pretty and sister of the moon,,
Who looks as if she is made of gold,
Who is saluted by all groups of sages,
Who grants salvation,
Who talks sweet words,
Who is praised by Vedas,
Who lives on the Lotus flower,
Who is worshipped by all devas,
Who showers good qualities on people,
And who is the personification of peace,
Please protect me always.

2. Dhanya Lakshmi [Lakshmi of Grains]:

Ayio kali kalmasha nasini, kamini,
Vaidhika roopini, veda maye,
Ksheera samudhbhava mangala roopini,
Manthra nivasini, manthranuthe,
Mangala dhayini, ambuja vasini,
deva ganarchitha padayuthe,
Jaya jaya he madhusoodhana kamini
Dhanyalakshmi sada palaya maam.

Victory and victory to Danyalakshmi
Oh darling of the killer of Madhu,
Who destroys bad effects of kali yuga,
Who is most desirable god,
Who is personification of Vedas,
Who is pervaded by the Vedas,
Who arose out of milk,
Who is the form of all that is good,
Who lives in the sacred chants,
Who lives on the lotus flower,
And whose feet is worshipped by devas,
Please protect me always

3. Dairya Lakshmi [Lakshmi of Courage]:

Jaya vara varnani, vaishnavi,
Bhargavi, manthra swaroopini, manthra maye,
Suragana poojitha seegra phala pradha ,
Jnana vikasini, sasthranuthe,
Bhava bhaya harini, papa vimochini,
Sadu janarchitha pada yuthe,

Jaya jaya he madhusoodhana kamini
Dairyalakshmi sada palaya maam.

Victory and victory to Dairyalakshmi
Oh, darling of the killer of Madhu,
Who is described by victorious and blessed,
Who is the shakthi which came out of Vishnu,
Who is the daughter of sage Bhargava,
Whose form is that of sacred chants,
Who is pervaded by sacred chants,
Who is worshipped by all devas,
Who gives results fast,
Who improves knowledge,
Who is worshipped by shastras,
Who destroys fear ,
Who gives redemption from sins,
And whose feet is worshipped by holy people,
Who lives on the lotus flower,
Please protect me always

4. Gaja Lakshmi [Lakshmi of Elephants]:

Jaya jaya durgathi nasini kamini,
Sarva phala pradha sastra maye,
Rathha gaja thuraga padathi samavrutha,
Parijana manditha lokanuthe,
Harihara brahma supoojitha sevitha ,
Thapa nivarini pada yuthe,
Jaya jaya he madhusoodhana kamini
Gajalakshmi sada palaya maam.

Victory and victory to Gajalakshmi
Oh darling of the killer of Madhu,
Victory and victory to you,
Who removes bad fate,
Who is desirable God,
Who is the personification of shastras,
Which bless one with all that is asked,
Who is surrounded by an army of elephants,
Chariots, horses and cavalry,
Who is worshipped and served by,
Shiva, Vishnu and Brahma,
And whose feet provides relief from suffering,
Please protect me always

5. Santana Lakshmi [Lakshmi of Progeny]:

Ayi kagha vahini, mohini, chakrini,
raga vivrdhni , jnanamaye,
Gunagana varidhi , loka hithaishini ,
Swara saptha bhooshitha gana nuthe,
Sakala surasura deva muneeswara ,
Manhava vandhitha padayuthe,
Jaya jaya he madhusoodhana kamini
Santhanaalakshmi sada palaya maam.

Victory and victory to Santhanalakshmi
Oh, darling of the killer of Madhu,
Who rides on the bird,
Who is an enchantress,
Who is the consort of he who holds the chakra,
Who pacifies emotions,
Who is pervaded by knowledge,

Who is ocean of good qualities,
Who has her mind in the good of all the world,
Who is worshipped by the music of seven swaras,
And who is worshipped by all devas, asuras,
Sages and all humans,
Please protect me always.

6. Vijaya Lakshmi [Lakshmi of Victory]:

Jaya kamalasini, sadgathi dayini,
jnana vikasini ganamaye,
Anudina marchitha kumkuma dhoosara
bhooshitha vaasitha vadhyanuthe,
Kanakadhara sthuthi vaibhava
vanditha shankara desika manyapathe,
Jaya jaya he madhusoodhana kamini
Vijayalakshmi sada palaya maam.

Victory and victory to Vijayalakshmi
The darling of the killer of Madhu,
Victory to she who sits on the lotus,
Who blesses us with salvation,
Who spreads our knowledge,
Who is pervaded with music,
Who is coated with the saffron powder,
Which is daily used to worship her,
Who is worshipped by playing of musical instruments,
And who was pleased by the prayer,
Of the golden rain by the great Sankara,
Please protect me always.

7. Vidhya Lakshmi [Lakshmi of Knowledge]:

Pranatha sureswari, bharathi, bhargavi
shoka vinasini, rathna maye,
Mani maya bhooshitha karma vibhooshana,
Santhi samavrutha hasyamukhe,
Nava nidhi dhayini kalimala harini,
Kamitha phalapradha hasthayuthe,
Jaya jaya he madhusoodhana kamini
Vidhyalakshmi sada palaya maam.

Victory and victory to Vidhyalakshmi
Oh, darling of the killer of Madhu,
Who is the pleased goddess of devas,
Who is he goddess of Bharatha,
Who is the daughter of sage Bhargava,
Who removes all sorrows,
Who is fully ornamented by precious stones,
Who wears several gem studded ornaments,
Whose ear is decorated,
Who is the abode of peace,
Who has a smiling face,
Who blesses us with nine types of wealth,
Who steals away bad effects of kali,
And whose hands blesses us,
For fulfillment of our wish,
Please protect me always

8. Dhana Lakshmi [Lakshmi of Wealth]:

Dhimidhimi dhindhimi dhindhimi dhindhimi,
dundubhi nada supoornamaye,
Ghumaghuma ghumaghuma ghumaghuma,
Sankha ninadha suvadhyanoothe,
Veda puranethihasa supoojitha,
Vaidhika marga pradarsayuthe,
Jaya jaya he madhusoodhana kamini
Danalakshmi sada palaya maam.

Victory and victory to Danalakshmi
Hey, darling of the killer of Madhu,
Who is fully complete with,
Dimidimi sounds of the drum,
And the majestic sound of conch,
Gumguma, ghummkuma, gunguma,
Who is worshipped by Vedas and puranas,
And who shows the path of religious discipline,
Please protect me always.

Maha Lakshmi Ashtakam

In the beginning of creation Lakshmi took form from the left side of Vishnu and was later born again from the sea of milk, when the devas churned it for getting nectar. She resides on the chest of Lord Vishnu as "Sri Vatsa". It was she who took birth as Sita when Vishnu incarnated as Rama. This simple prayer is very ancient and has been chanted by generations for solving all their problems.

1
Namosthesthu Maha Maye,
Sree peede, sura poojithe,
Sanka , chakra, Gadha hasthe,
Maha Lakshmi Namosthuthe.

Salutations and salutations to Goddess Mahalakshmi,
Who is the great enchantress,
Who lives in riches,
Who is worshipped by Gods,
And who has conch, wheel and mace in her hands.

2
Namasthe garudarude,
Kolasura bhayam kari,
Sarva papa hare , devi,
Maha Lakshmi Namosthuthe.

Salutations and salutations to Goddess Mahalakshmi.
Who rides on an eagle,
Who created fear to Kolasura,
And is the goddess who can destroy all sins

3
Sarvagne Sarva varadhe,
Sarva dushta Bhayam karee,
Sarva dukha hare, devi,
Maha Lakshmi Namosthuthe.

Salutations and salutations to Goddess Mahalakshmi.
Who knows everything,
Who can grant any thing,
Who appears fearsome to bad people,
And is the goddess who can destroy all sorrows.

4
Sidhi budhi pradhe devi,
Bhakthi mukthi pradayinee,
Manthra moorthe, sada devi,
Maha Lakshmi Namosthuthe.

Salutations and salutations to Goddess Mahalakshmi,
Who grants intelligence and occult powers,
Who grants devotion to God and salvation,
Who can be personified by holy chants,
And who is Goddess for ever.

5
Adhyantha rahithe, devi,
Adhi Shakthi maheswari,
Yogaje yoga sambhoothe,
Maha Lakshmi Namosthuthe.

Salutations and salutations to Goddess Mahalakshmi.
Who neither has an end nor beginning,

Who is the primeval power,
Who is the greatest Goddess,
Who is born out of hard penance,
And who can be personified by meditation.

6
Sthoola Sukshma maha roudhre,
Maha Shakthi Maho dhare,
Maha papa hare devi,
Maha Lakshmi Namosthuthe.

Salutations and salutations to Goddess Mahalakshmi,
Who is micro and also gross,
Who is most fearsome ,
Who is the greatest strength,
Who within her holds the worlds,
And is the Goddess who can destroy sins.

7
Padmasana sthithe, devi,
Para brahma swaroopini,
Para mesi, jagan matha,
Maha Lakshmi Namosthuthe.

Salutations and salutations to Goddess Mahalakshmi,
Who is the goddess who has the seat of Lotus,
Who is the personification of the ultimate truth,
Who is Goddess of all,
And who is the mother of all the worlds.

8
Swethambara dhare, devi,
Nanalankara bhooshithe,
Jagat sthithe, jagan matha,
Maha Lakshmi Namosthuthe.

Salutations and salutations to Goddess Mahalakshmi,
Who wears white cloth,
Who wears variety of ornaments,
Who is everywhere in the world,
And who is the mother of all the worlds.

Phala Sruthi

Maha lakmyashtakam stotram,
Ya padeth Bhakthiman nara,
Sarva sidhi mavapnothi,
Rajyam prapnothi sarvadha.

Those men who read this octet praising Mahalakshmi,
With devotion and discipline,
Would make all powers as his own,,
And also would attain the kingdom for ever.

Maha Lakshmi Stotram

Lakshmi is the goddess of wealth. Wealth does not mean only money or assets in Hinduism. It has several aspects. Goddess Lakshmi divides herself intos everal such aspects to grace the devotee. This prayer is to 15 such aspects of Goddess Lakshmi.

1
Adhi Lakshmi namosthesthu,
Para brahma swaroopini,
Yaso dehi, danam dehi,
Sarva Kamamscha dehi mey. 1

I salute Primeval Lakshmi,
Who is personification of eternal truth.
Please give me fame, give me wealth,
And also fulfill all my desires.

2
Santhana Lakshmi namosthesthu,
Puthra pouthra pradayini,
Puthraan dehi, danam dehi,
Sarva kamamscha dehi mey.

I salute Santhana Lakshmi,
Who grants sons and grand sons.
Please give me sons and wealth,
And also fulfill all my desires.

3
Vidhya Lakshmi namosthesthu,
Brahma vidhya swaroopini,
Vidhyam dehi, kalam dehi,
Sarva kamamscha dehi mey.

I salute Vidhya Lakshmi,
Who is personification of eternal knowledge.
Give me learning, give me arts,
And also fulfill all my desires.

4
Dhana Lakshmi namosthesthu
Sarva daridrya nasini,
Danam dehi, sriyam dehi,
Sarva kamamscha dehi mey.

I salute Dhana Lakshmi,
Who destroys all types of poverty,
Give me wealth, Give me opulence,
And also fulfill all my desires.

5
Danya Lakshmi namosthesthu.
Sarvaabharana bhooshithe,
Danyam dehi, danam dehi,
Sarva kamamscha dehi mey.

I salute Danya Lakshmi,
Who wears all type of ornaments.

Please give me cereals and wealth,
And also fulfill all my desires.

6
Medha Lakshmi namosthesthu,
Kali kalmasha naasini,
Pragnaam dehi, sriyam dehi,
Sarva kamamscha dehi mey.

I salute Medha Lakshmi,
Who destroys even effects of kali.
Give me knowledge and wealth,
And also fulfill all my desires.

7
Gaja Lakshmi namosthesthu,
Sarva deva swaroopini,
Aswam cha gokulam dehi,
Sarva kamamscha dehi mey.

I salute Gaja Lakshmi,
Who is personification of all gods.
Give me horses and hoards of cattle,
And also fulfill all my desires.

8
Veera Lakshmi namosthesthu,
Para shakthi swaroopini,
Veeryam dehi, balam Devi,
Sarva kamamscha dehi mey.

I salute Veera Lakshmi,
Who is personification of eternal power.
Give me heroism and strength,
And also fulfill all my desires.

9
Jaya Lakshmi namosthesthu,
Sarva karya jaya pradhe,
Jayam dehi, shubham dehi,
Sarva kamamscha dehi mey.

I salute Jaya Lakshmi,
Who is victory in all matters.
Give me victory and good,
And also fulfill all my desires.

10
Bhagya Lakshmi namosthesthu,
Soumangalya vivardhani,
Bhagyam dehi, sriyam dehi,
Sarva kamamscha dehi mey.

I salute Bhagya Lakshmi,
Who grants holiness,
Please give me luck and wealth,
And also fulfill all my desires

11
Keerthi Lakshmi namosthesthu,
Vishnu vaksha sthala sthithe,
Keerthim dehi, sriyam dehi,
Sarva kamamscha dehi mey.

I salute Keerthi Lakshmi,
Who resides on the chest of Vishnu.
Please give me fame and wealth,
And also fulfill all my desires.

12
Aarogya Lakshmi namosthesthu,
Sarva roga nivaarini,
Ayur dehi, sriyam dehi,
Sarva kamamscha dehi mey.

I salute Aarogya Lakshmi,
Who cures all diseases.
Please give me long life and wealth,
And also fulfill all my desires.

13
Sidha Lakshmi namosthesthu,
Sarva sidhi pradhayani,
Sidhim dehi, sriyam dehi,
Sarva kamamscha dehi mey.

I salute Sidha Lakshmi,
Who grants all occult powers.

Please give me occult powers and wealth,
And also fulfill all my desires.

14
Soundarya Lakshmi namosthesthu,
Sarvalangara shobithe,
Roopam dehi sriyam dehi,
Sarva kamamscha dehi mey.

I salute Soundarya Lakshmi,
Who shines with all types of decoration.
Please give me beauty and wealth,
And also fulfill all my desires.

15
Samrajya Lakshmi namosthesthu,
Bhukthi mukthi pradhayani,
Moksham dehi sriyam dehi.
Sarva kamamscha dehi mey.

I salute Samrajya Lakshmi,
Who provides independence and salvation.
Please give me salvation and wealth,
And also fulfill all my desires.

16
Mangale mangaladhre,
Mangalye mangalapradhe,
Mangalartham mangalesi,
Mangalyam dehi mey sada.

Oh Goddess who is good, who is the basis of good,
Who forever lives with her husband and who does good,
For the sake of good, Oh goddess who does good,
Always give long life to my husband.

17
Sarva mangala mangalye, Shive, sarvartha sadhake,
Saranye triambike Gowri narayani namosthuthe.

Oh Goddess who is a giver of all good things, who is peaceful,
Who is a giver of all wealth, who can be relied upon,
Who has three eyes and who is golden in colour,
Our salutations to you, Narayani

18
Shubham bhavathu kalyani ayur arogya sampadham,
Mama shathru vinaasaya, deepa jyothi namo nama.

Salutations and salutations to the flame of the lamp,
Let all good things happen, let us have long life with health,

And please destroy all my enemies.

Lakshmi Astotara Shantanam Stotram
This was given by Lord Shiva to Parvati.

Sri Devyuvacha
Devadeva mahadeva trikalajna maheshvara
Karunakara devesha bhaktanugrahakaraka 1
Ashtottarashatam lakshmyah shrotumichchhami tattvataha

Ishvara uvacha
Devi sadhu mahabhage mahabhagyapradayakam
Sarvaishvaryakaram punyam sarvapapapranashanam 2

Sarvadaridryashamanam shravanadbhuktimuktidam
Rajavashyakaram divyam guhyadguhyatamam param 3

Durlabham sarvadevanam chatuhshashtikalaspadam
Padmadinam varantanam vidhinam nityadayakam   4

Samastadevasa.nsevyamanimadyashtasiddhidam
Kimatra bahunoktena devi pratyakshadayakam   5

Tava prityadya vakshyami samahitamanah shrrinum
Ashtottarashatasyasya mahalakshmistu devata 6

Klimbijapadamityuktam shaktistu bhuvaneshvari
Anganyasah karanyasa sa ityadih prakirtitah 7

Dhyanam
Vande padmakaram prasannavadanam saubhagyadam bhagyadam
Hastabhyamabhayapradam maniganairnanavidhairbhushitam

Bhaktabhishtaphalapradam hariharabrahmadibhih sevitam
Parshve pankajashankhapadmanidhibhiryuktam sada shaktibhih   8

Sarasijanayane sarojahaste dhavalatara.nshukagandhamalyashobhe
Bhagavati harivallabhe manojne tribhuvanabhutikari prasida
mahyam   9

Prakritim vikritim vidyam sarvabhutahitapradam
Shraddham vibhutim surabhim namami paramatmikam   10

Vacham padmalayam padmam shuchim svaham svadham sudham
Dhanyam hiranmayim lakshmim nityapushtam vibhavarim   11

Aditim cha ditim diptam vasudham vasudharinim
Namami kamalam kantam kamakshim krodhasambhavam   12

Anugrahapadam buddhimanagham harivallabham
Ashokamamritam diptam lokashokavinashinim   13

Namami dharmanilayam karunam lokamataram
Padmapriyam padmahastam padmakshim padmasundarim   14

Padmodbhavam padmamukhim padmanabhapriyam ramam
Padmamaladharam devim padminim padmagandhinim   15

Punyagandham suprasannam prasadabhimukhim prabham
Namami chandravadanam chandram chandrasahodarim   16

Chaturbhujam chandrarupamindiramindushitalam
Ahladajananim pushtim shivam shivakarim satim   17

Vimalam vishvajananim tushtim daridryanashinim
Pritipushkarinim shantam shuklamalyambaram shriyam   18

Bhaskarimm bilvanilayam vararoham yashasvinim
Vasundharamudarangim harinim hemamalinim   19

Dhanadhanyakarim siddhim sada saumyam shubhapradam
Nripaveshmagatanandam varalakshmim vasupradam   20

Shubham hiranyaprakaram samudratanayam jayam
Namami mangalam devim vishnuvakshahsthalasthitam   21

Vishnupatnim prasannakshim narayanasamashritam
Daridryadhva.nsinim devim sarvopadravaharinim   22

Navadurgam mahakalim brahmavishnushivatmikam
Trikalajnanasampannam namami bhuvaneshvarim   23

Lakshmim kshirasamudrarajatanayam shrirangadhameshvarim
Dasibhutasamastadevavanitam lokaikadipankuram

Shrimanmandakatakshalabdhavibhavabrahmendra gangadharam

Tvam Trailokyakutumbinim sarasijam vande mukundapriyam   24

Matarnamami kamale kamalayatakshi
Shrivishnuhritkamalavasini vishvamatah
Kshirodaje kamalakomalagarbhagauri lakshmi
Prasida satatam namatam sharanye   25

Phala Shruti Shloka

Trikalam yo japedvidvan shanmasam vijitendriyah
Daridryadhva.nsanam kritva sarvamapnotyayatnatah 26

Devinamasahasreshu punyamashtottaram shatam
Yena shriyamavapnoti kotijanmadaridratah 27

Bhriguvare shatam dhiman pathedvatsaramatrakam
Ashtaishvaryamavapnoti kubera iva bhutale 28

Daridryamochanam nama stotramambaparam shatam |
Yena shriyamavapnoti kotijanmadaridritah 29

Bhuktva tu vipulan bhoganasyah sayujyamapnuyat
Pratahkale pathennityam sarvaduhkhopashantaye
Pathanstu chintayeddevim sarvabharanabhushitam 30

Iti Shri Lakshmi Astotara Shatanama Stotram Sampurnam

Lakshmi Stuti

Indra said:

Namaste Sarva-Lokanam-Jananeem Ambaj-Sambhavam Sriyam - Unindra-Padma-Akshim Vishnu-Vaksha-Sthala-Sthitam

Padma-Aalyam Padma-Karim Padma-Patra-Nibhekhnaam Vande Padma-Mukheem Deveem Padma-Nabha-Priyaam Aham

Tvam Siddhis Tvam Svadha Svaha Sudha Tvam Lok-Pavani Sandhya Ratri Prabha Bhootir Medha Sraddha Sarasvati

Yagya-Vidya Maha-Vidya Guhya-Vidhya Cha Shobhane Aatma-Vidya Cha Devi Tvam Vimukti-Phal-Dayani

Aanveekhikee Trayee Vaarta Danda-Neeti TvamEva Cha Saumya-Asaumyar Jagad-Roopais TvaEtad Devi Pooritam

Ka Tv Anya Tvam Rte Devi Sarva-Yajya-Mayam Vapuhu Adhyaaste Dev-Devasya Yogi Chintyam Gada-bhrit

Tvaya Devi Parityaktam Sakalam Bhuvan-Tryam Vinishta Prayam ABhavat Tvedaaneem Samedhitam

Dara Purtaas Tatha gaar Suhrid Dhanya Dhan Aadikam Bhavatyetan Maha-Bhage Nityam Tvad-Veekshnaan-Nrinaam
Shareer-Arogyam Aishvaryam Ari-Paksha-Kshaya Sukham Devi Tvad-Drishti-Drishtaanam Purushaanaam Na Durlabham

Tvam Mata Sarva-Lokanam Deva-Devo-Hari Pitah TvaEtad Vishnuna Cha Amb Jagad Vyaptam Chara-Acharam

Ma Nah Kosham Tatha Goshtam Ma Graham Ma Parichedam Ma Shareeram Kalatram Cha Tyajethah Sarva-Pavani

Ma Puran ma Suhrid-Varga Ma Pashun ma Vibhushanam Tyajetha Mam Devasya Vishnor-Vaksha-Sthala-Aalye

Sattven Satya Shauchaabhyam Tatha Sheela Aadibhir Gunaih Tyajyante Te Narah Sadhyah Santyaktaa Ye Tvaya Amale

Tvaya Vilokita Sadhya Sheela Aadyair Akhilair Gunai Kula Aishvaryash cha Yujante Purusha Nirguna Api

Sa Shlaaghya Sa Guni Dhanyah Sa Kuleenah Sa Buddhiman Sa Shurah Sa cha Vikranto Yas Tvaya Devi Vikshitah

Sadhyo Vaigunyam ayanti Sheeladyaah Saklaa Gunaah ParanMukhee Jagad-Dhatree Yasya Tvam Vishnu-Vallabhe

Na Te Varnyitum Shakta Gunaan Jihvaa Api Vedhsah Praseed Devi Padma-Akshi Ma Asmaans Tyaaksheeh Kadaachan

Meaning in English

I bow to you, O Mother of All Worlds, O Lotus Born, the one with eyes like lotus petals, sitting on the chest of Vishnu.

Sitting on a lotus, lotus-like hands, and eyes like lotus petals, Praised be you, O Lotus faced Devi.

You are Siddhi, Svadha, Svaha, Sudha. You are the purifier of this world. You are the evening, the night, the light. You are Glory, intelligence, devotion. You are Sarasvati.

You are Yagya Vidya (the knowdlege of Yajya), you are the great knowdlege, the secret knowledge, O Auspicious. You are the science of the self, O Devi, and you are the giver of the fruit of Mukti (freedom).

Logic, the knowledge of all Vedas, worldly knowdlege, and Raja Neeti are all you. You are fully filled and are present every where in this world with your peaceful and fierce forms.

O Devi, who other than you could reside in the heart of the him who is the real form of all Yajyas, who is contemplated by all Gods, and Yogis, and who bears a mace.

O Devi. When you give up these entire 3 worlds, this entire creation goes to destruction, and you yourself have again given life to it.

By your grace only, a person gets a wife, son, house, wealth, prosperity and friends.
Those on whom you you bestow your kindness, good health, prosperity, destruction of enemies, and happiness are not hard to attain.

You are the mother of these entire worlds, and the God of Gods, Sri Hari are the father. You and Vishnu, O Mother are present every where in this moving and unmoving creation.

Please never leave our wealth, animal-houses, home, enjoyables, body, wife etc. O Vishnu-Vaksha-Stal-Vaasini, never leave our sons, friends, animals and jewels.

Please never leave our wealth, animal-houses, home, enjoyables, body, wife etc. O Vishnu-Vaksha-Stal-Vaasini, never leave our sons, friends, animals and jewels.

O Pure, when you leave a person, his purity, truthfulness, cleanliness and good behaviour etc. goodness also leave him in no time.

And by your kind grace, even virtueless people very soon become full of virtues and goodness, prosperity etc.

The one of whom you bestow your kind look, is admirable, is virtuous, is fortunate, is full of goodness, is intelligent, and he is brave and oppulent.

O Dear to Vishnu, O mother of this world, the one who is left by you, all his virtues become vices immediately.

O Devi, even Sri Brahma Ji is not capable of praising your greatness. Thus, please be satisfied with us and don't leave us ever.

Benefits

The text of Vishnu Purana describes that after reciting this prayer, Sri Parashar said:

Thus praised by Indra, the omni present Lakshmi Ji said this to Indra, in the presence of all Gods: I am satisfied by this prayer of yours, O king of gods. I have come here to bestow on you a wish - ask for a wish.

Indra said: O Devi, if you want to give me a wish, and if I am qualified enough for your wish, then O Devi, please never give up these 3-worlds. Also, please grant me another wish: Who ever praises you with this stotra, never leave him, O one who appeared from the ocean. Those who read it every day, Lakshmi never leaves their homes.

Sri said:
O Vasav (Indra), I shall not leave this world. Being satisfied with your worshipping me through this prayer, I give you this wish: whichever human being, in evening or morning, praises me with this Stotra, I shall never leave him in the future.

Sri Parashar said:
This, in former time, satisfied with this Stotra's worship, Mahabhaga Sri (Sri Lakshmi Ji) gave these boons to the king of Gods.

Thus I have told you the story of appearance of Lakshmi:
When ever, the ruler of this world, God of Gods, Sri Janardhan, appear as an Avatar, Sri also appears then. When Sri Hari appeared as Aditya, Lakshmi Ji appeared as Padma.

When Sri Hari appeared as Parashurama, Lakshmi appeared as Prithvi. When Sri Hari appeared as Raam (Raaghav), Lakshmi become Sita, and when Sri Hari took birth as Krishna, Lakshmi manifested as Rukmani. In other Avatars too, Lakshmi is never separated from Sri Vishnu.

If he takes a divine form, she takes a divine form. And on taking a human form, she takes a human form. She takes her form according to the form of Sri Vishnu.

Whoever listens or reads the story of the birth of Sri Lakshmi in his home, Sri always stays.

In homes in which is read this stuti of Sri Lakshmi (Indra's Stuti), in that home, the root of all suffering, poverty never remains.

This I have told, the giver of all prosperity, glory and richness, this Stuti of Sri Lakshmi, that appeared from the mouth of Indra.

Lakshmi ashtottara shatanamavali

108 names of the Divine Mother Lakshmi

Om prakrityai namah .

Om vikrityai namah .

Om vidyaayai namah .

Om sarvabhuutahitapradaayai namah .

Om shraddhaayai namah .

Om vibhuutyai namah .

Om surabhyai namah .

Om paramaatmikaayai namah .

Om vaache namah .

Om padmaalayaayai namah .

Om padmaayai namah .

Om shuchaye namah .

Om svaahaayai namah .

Om svadhaayai namah .

Om sudhaayai namah .

Om dhanyaayai namah .

Om hiranmayyai namah .

Om laxmyai namah .

Om nityapushhtaayai namah .

Om vibhaavaryai namah .

Om adityai namah .

Om ditye namah .

Om diipaayai namah .

Om vasudhaayai namah .

Om vasudhaarinyai namah .

Om kamalaayai namah .

Om kaantaayai namah .

Om kaamaaxyai namah .

Om krodhasambhavaayai namah .

Om anugrahapradaayai namah .

Om buddhaye namah .

Om anaghaayai namah .

Om harivallabhaayai namah .

Om ashokaayai namah .

Om amritaayai namah .

Om diiptaayai namah .

Om lokashokavinaashinyai namah .

Om dharmanilayaayai namah .

Om karunaayai namah .

Om lokamaatre namah .

Om padmapriyaayai namah .

Om padmahastaayai namah .

Om padmaaxyai namah .

Om padmasundaryai namah .

Om padmodbhavaayai namah .

Om padmamukhyai namah .

Om padmanaabhapriyaayai namah .

Om ramaayai namah .

Om padmamaalaadharaayai namah .

Om devyai namah .

Om padminyai namah .

Om padmagandhinyai namah .

Om punyagandhaayai namah .

Om suprasannaayai namah .

Om prasaadaabhimukhyai namah .

Om prabhaayai namah .

Om chandravadanaayai namah .

Om chandraayai namah .

Om chandrasahodaryai namah .

Om chaturbhujaayai namah .

Om chandraruupaayai namah .

Om indiraayai namah .

Om indushiitalaayai namah .

Om aahlaadajananyai namah .

Om pushhtayai namah .

Om shivaayai namah .

Om shivakaryai namah .

Om satyai namah .

Om vimalaayai namah .

Om vishvajananyai namah .

Om tushhtayai namah .

Om daaridryanaashinyai namah .

Om priitipushhkarinyai namah .

Om shaantaayai namah .

Om shuklamaalyaambaraayai namah .

Om shriyai namah .

Om bhaaskaryai namah .

Om bilvanilayaayai namah .

Om varaarohaayai namah .

Om yashasvinyai namah .

Om vasundharaayai namah .

Om udaaraa.ngaayai namah .

Om harinyai namah .

Om hemamaalinyai namah .

Om dhanadhaanyakarye namah .

Om siddhaye namah .

Om strainasaumyaayai namah .

Om shubhapradaaye namah .

Om nripaveshmagataanandaayai namah .

Om varalaxmyai namah .

Om vasupradaayai namah .

Om shubhaayai namah .

Om hiranyapraakaaraayai namah .

Om samudratanayaayai namah .

Om jayaayai namah .

Om mangalaa devyai namah .

Om vishhnuvaxassthalasthitaayai namah .

Om vishhnupatnyai namah .

Om prasannaaxyai namah .

Om naaraayanasamaashritaayai namah .

Om daaridryadhv.nsinyai namah .

Om devyai namah .

Om sarvopadrava vaarinyai namah .

Om navadurgaayai namah .

Om mahaakaalyai namah .

Om brahmaavishhnushivaatmikaayai namah .

Om trikaalagyaanasampannaayai namah .

Om bhuvaneshvaryai namah .

Practice #2

Mantra

One of the great paths of liberation is by the practice of mantras or spiritually charged sonic patterns formed from the Sanskrit language.

The word *mantram* combines the root *manas* (mind) with *tram* (protection) so the literal meaning is mind-protection. The mind is subject to innumerable perturbations that constantly disturb and keep it from the stillness that can lead the soul to higher consciousness. The proper practice of a mantra will lead the soul to the realization of the Self.

Since the effectiveness of mantras depend on their vibrations, their correct pronunciation become very important. They can be practiced by chanting aloud or by repeating mentally – some of them are meant to be mentally repeated for the purpose of being internalized, while others give emphasis to external effects. Mantras have been known to promote self-healing, spiritual development, as well as beneficial effects on the world around us.

Mantras can be used as the only means of spiritual liberation or as part of an integrated yogic system. Most yogic paths utilize some form of mantra or another in their techniques.

The most basic mantra is Om which is known as the "pranava mantra," the source of all mantras. It is the humming sound of creation because it is the vibration of the universe and the sound uttered by the Divine Creatrix. More complex sound patterns utilize the sound of Om in their beginning. It is used as an address for the Divine.

Om is the principal mantra given by Patanjali in his Yoga Sutras. It can be chanted aloud, whispered or repeated mentally. In higher yogic techniques, instead of repeating the sound, the student should listen and try to hear the sound within and without – forming a powerful connection with the Universal Soul.

Nowadays, the emphasis is on the mantras which utilize bija or seed sounds because of their easier pronunciation, and prevalent use in tantric systems. Mantras were originally conceived in the ancient scriptures known as the Vedas. When they are crafted into two-line verses, they are called "shlokas."

The Lakshmi mantras connect with the vibrations of prosperity and success. Just as we can tune into different radio stations, we can attune ourselves with different aspects of the Divine.

Practice of the Lakshmi Mantras:
Choose one of the following mantras and repeat 108 times in the morning and 108 times in the evening.

The repetition of 108 times is done with the first 36 repetitions aloud in a normal voice, 36 times in a whisper and the last 36 times silently.

Lakshmi Bija Mantra

Shreem

"*Sh*" represents the transcendent Divinity of Fortune
"*r*" represents wealth
"*ee*" represents satisfaction
"*m*" represents the dispelling of sorrow

Lakshmi Gayatri Mantra

**Om mahadevyiyai ca vidmahe
visnupatnyai ca dhimahi
tanno lakshmih prachodayat**

Rig Veda MahaaLakshmi Mantra

Om Shreem hreem shreem
Kamale kamalaalaye praseeda praseeda
shreem hreem shreem om
Shri mahaalakshmi devyai namaha

Suabhagya Lakshmi Mantra

Om Shreem hreem kleem em
kamala vaasinyai svaahaa

Diwali (Deepvali) - the festival of lights

Celebration : October, after five days of Mahadashami.

The Festival
Lakshmi Puja is the most important festival for most Indian families. Lakshmi is the Goddess of light, beauty, good fortune and wealth,prosperity, success and knowledge.

Timing of the year
In the month of October, five days after Mahadashami, on the day of the full moon, is the festival of the Goddess of prosperity Laxmi who is worshipped daily in most Hindu household for the family's well being. Public Pujas are performed in many premises.

On this day the people worship the Goddess of wealth, Lakshmi. The statues or images of Lakshmi are installed and specially prepared cakes made of fruits and sweets are offered to the goddess. During the night, celebrations are usually spent in the open singing and dancing - generally getting together in the cool bright moonlight.

Lakshmi Puja
The day of Lakshmi Puja falls on the dark night of Amabasya. Lakshmi Puja is celebrated in the evening when tiny diyas or clay lamps are lit to drive away the shadows of evil spirits. Devotional songs in praise of Goddess Lakshmi are sung and traditional sweets are offered to the Goddess.

It is believed that on this day Lakshmi walks through the green fields and loiters through the bye-lanes and showers her blessings on man and woman with plenty and prosperity.

Story of Lakshmi Puja

There are various explanations for the celebration of Diwali.

It is believed that when the demons and deities were churning the ocean together to recover the 'drink of immortality', it was on this day that Goddess Lakshmi manifested herself and thus Lakshmi Puja is celebrated to commemorate the birth of the Goddess of Wealth.

According to another legend, on the night prior to the celebration of Diwali, Lord Krishna killed the demon Narakasura, freeing the earth from his terrors and liberating the 16000 princesses that were abducted by him. Thus, on the next day (Diwali), the people illuminated their houses and celebrated to express their joy and relief. The ancient tale of Mahabharata mentions the return of the Pandavas to their kingdom from their 13-year long exile on this very day.

Vikramaditya, the great benevolent king and warrior was believed to be enthroned on Diwali. Whatever the reasons may be, however, Diwali, has always been associated with the worshipping of Lakshmi.

One other legend connecting Lakshmi to Diwali is mentioned in Sanatkumar Samhita, which says that it was on this day that Lord Vishnu liberated his consort from the captivity of Bali, the mighty demon-king after a long period.

Another popular tradition is that Diwali celebrates the return of Rama, the divine Avatar of Lord Vishnu, after 14 years of exile during which he lost and rescued his wife Sita and defeated the demon king Ravana. The people of Ayodhya lit lamps to light the way and to celebrate his return.

The festival of five days

The festival of Deepawali is always celebrated in October or November, when the rainy season has completely finished. Traditionally, it is considered as a five-day celebration, each day with its own significance.

Day 1: Dhanterus: The celebration begins from the day of Dhanterus, two days before Diwali that bring good fortune and prosperity. Dhanterus is regarded as the birth day of god Dhanvantari, who also arose during the churning of the great ocean by the gods and the asuras. Dhanterus means Dhan+terus, in which Dhan denotes money and terus is the thirteenth day of the month. It is also known as Dhanvantri Jayanti or Dhantrayodasi because of the birth day of god Dhanvantri, the god of health and ayurveda. On this day people buy utensils and jewellery for performing traditional ceremonies, as it is believed to be a symbol of good fortune.

Day 2: Naraka Chaturdashi: The second day of Diwali is known as Naraka Chaturdashi, the fourteenth day of the month on which demon Narakasura was killed. It signifies the victory of good over evil and light over darkness. It is the prime day of the festival in south India. The people perform puja of Lord Sri Krishna or Lord Sri Vishnu. The people enlighten the 'Diya' (earthen lamp) before the main door of their homes on this day. This day is also known as Roop Chaturdashi.

Day 3: Lakshmi Puja: In the north of India, the third day of this festival is the most important day on which the goddess of wealth, Lakshmi and God of fortune, Ganesha are worshipped by all. People enlighten the earthen lamps across the streets and homes, and pray for their prosperity and well-beings. Children play fireworks and massive crackers are fired to express their joy on this day.

Day 4: Govardhan Puja : The day after the prime day of Diwali is known as Govardhan Puja or Annakut. On this day Lord Krishna defeated Indra by lifting Govardhan Mountain on his little finger. On the other hand, Annakut denotes a mountain of food that is decorated as a symbol of Govardhan Mountain. The people present gifts to their wives on this day.

Day 5: Bhaiduj (also Bhayyaduj, Bhaubeej or Bhayitika) : The last day is for an auspicious relationship of brothers and sisters, especially married brothers and sisters. Brothers and sisters express their love and affection for each other by tying a thread. This festival is very similar to the festival of Raksha Bandhan.

Practice #3

Introduction to Puja

The invocation ceremony for the divine is know as Puja. It is conducted to a statue/vigraha made of gold, silver, bronze or even clay. Those who do not have statues can utilize paintings/pictures or an abstract representation such as yantra. Before the puja, one bathes to signify the outer purification. Mantras and stotras are recited for inner purification.

A puja is always done in a special place in a room. Many different sacred items can be kept in the puja room and used during the ceremony like vigrahas (statues), incense, meditation oils, and chanting books or chalisas. Every object associated with the ritual of Puja is symbolically significant.

Puja Requirements

A small bench or a wooden table or a cardboard box covering an area no larger than 36" x 24" and about 15" to 24" tall is adequate. The size can vary if you wish to arrange more or fewer pictures and/or statues on the surface. Remember that you should be able to see the items on the altar and have easy access to make offerings during the ceremony.

Place the table (or box) against a wall and cover it with a clean cloth, preferably white, and secure the same by tucking it under so that it won't slip off easily. Tape it on if necessary such that the tape is not visible.

The image/picture of the deity, which is called 'vigraha' (Sanskrit: 'vi' + 'graha') means something that is devoid of the ill effects of the planets or 'grahas', must also be arranged on the altar in a way that it leans against the wall.

Prepare one or two lamps with cotton wicks soaking in oil. Place the lamp(s) about 6 inches in front of the picture if it is one lamp, or about 10 inches apart if two lamps. Do not light these until you are ready to begin the Puja. Please note that it is ideal to light two wicks in the lamps, one facing the dieties and the other towards you. The lamp we light represents the light in us, that is the soul, which we offer to the Absolute.

Prepare a unused plate (stainless steel, silver or any other metal) by placing on it small vessels (cup-like, preferably metallic) of kumkum (vermilion), turmeric, one packet of camphor, sandal paste, a dozen agarbatti sticks (incense sticks) and a match box. The incense we burn collectively stands for the desires we have for various things in life. The vermilion or red powder stands for our emotions.

Prepare another plate, 12 inches or 24 inches in diameter. It can be metallic or wicker and put a variety of fruits (bananas, apples, oranges, etc.) and a couple of varieties of leaves and flowers. The flowers that we offer to the deity stands for the good that has blossomed in us. The fruits offered symbolize our detachment, self-sacrifice and surrender - the fruits of our actions.

You will need an aarati plate. This can be a small plate with a few vertical wicks soaking in oil or ghee or an aarati receptacle with a few wicks soaking in oil or ghee.

You will also need a small cup of akshata (raw unbroken rice).

Covered dishes of your favorite prasaadam or sweets may be placed in front of the altar on the cloth covered ground. A metallic vessel large enough to contain a couple of mugs of water should be filled with water and placed in front of the altar. You will need a smaller vessel, preferably a metallic straight-walled tumbler into which water will be poured during the service.

A dispenser (called uddharana or a simple metallic spoon) to dispense water from the tumbler will be needed. You will need a piece of colorful cloth for the Goddess.

Now you are ready to begin. Light the lamps and a couple of incense sticks. Keep them safely in the vicinity such that they present no hazard. Direct the agarbatti smoke towards the altar such that the smoke does not cause discomfort with chanting.

You must realize that in a few moments you will be invoking and receiving a divine energy and therefore the principal mood should be one of joy and devotion, but the mind should be relaxed. Make sure nothing starts until you are certain that a pleasant, sincere, reverential, relaxed environment is created to fill yourselves with joy as you begin to surrender to the divine power of Lakshmi.

Lakshmi Puja Ritual Outline

- Firstly lay a new cloth on a raised platform and then place a handful of grains in the center of the cloth and on the top of these grains situate a kalash or pitcher, which can be made up of gold, silver or copper.

- Then fill the three fourth of kalash with water and lay a betel nut, some flowers, some rice grain and a coin in it. Now arrange five kinds of leaves in the kalash. Cover the kalash with a small plate filled with rice grains.

- A lotus flower needs to be drawn over the rice grains with turmeric powder (haldi); then place the image of the goddess Lakshmi on the flower along with some coins.

- Now place the statue of lord Ganesha in the southwest direction of goddess Lakshmi, in front of the kalash.

- Initiate the Lakshmi Puja by offering haldi, kumkum and flowers to the images of lord Ganesha and goddess Lakshmi. Next offer these things to the water to be used for the Lakshmi Puja. Through these offerings invoke the river goddess to be a part of this water.

- Invoke the goddess Lakshmi with the help of power chants and mantras addressed to the goddess. If you don't know the mantras (refer to previous sections) then simply close your eyes, take some water in your hands and think of divine Lakshmi and finally offer the flowers to her image.

- Next, place the image of goddess Lakshmi in a clean plate and bathe it with water, panchamrit that is a mixture of milk, curd, ghee and sugar and finally with water having some gold ornament or even a pearl. Wipe the image clean and lay it back on the kalash.

- Make the offerings of sandal paste, saffron paste, perfume, kumkum, haldi and gulal(rose) to the image Now make an offer of a garland of cotton beads to both of the images of lord Ganesha and goddess Lakshmi.

- Offer the flowers, like the marigold flowers or leaves of bel, which is a wood apple tree. Also make an offering of some sweets, coconut and fruits. Remember to light an incense stick and dhoop in front of the two images.

- Now pour some puffed rice, batasha, cumin seeds and coriander seeds in front of the images.

- Complete the Lakshmi Puja by performing an aarti for goddess Lakshmi and lord Ganesha. Take care to ring a small bell while singing the aarti and it should not be accompanied with claps as is the practice adopted for other divine beings.

The complete Puja requires over one hour and requires the repetition of the at least one of the the stotras given in practice #1 and all the mantras given in practice #2, as well as the aarti given in practice #4. It is usually done during Deepwali.

A shorter symbolic version, suitable to be done on Fridays is given next.

Short Puja (2-5 minutes)

Each time when you say 'Samarpayami' (literally: I am offering), please offer two akshathas to the Mother with love and devotion.

Akshatha is uncooked rice, if possible colored with kumkum or red powder, saffron powder, tumeric and a little bit of water. A bowl of this colored rice can be prepared in advance and kept near the altar.

1. **Dhyaanam Samarpayami** :
   think or meditate on Lakshmi

2. **Aawaahanam Samarpayami**:
   offering invitation to Lakshmi

3. **Aasanam Samarpayami**:
   offer a seat to Lakshmi

4. **Paadyam Samarpayami**:
   offer water to wash Her feet

5. **Arghyam Samarpayami**:
   offer water to wash Her hands

6. **Aachamaneeyam Samarpayami**:
   offer water to drink

7. **Snaanam Samarpayami**:
   give bath to Lakshmi

8. **Maha Abhishekam Samarpayami**:
   main head bath

9. **Pratishtaapayaami**:
   establish Her seat

10. **Vasthram Samarpayami**:
    offer clothes to Lakshmi

11. **Yajnopaveetham Samarpayami**:
    offer the Holy Thread to Lakshmi

12. **Gandham Samarpayami**:
    offer sandlewood paste / powder

13. **Akshatham Samarpayami**:
    offer Akshatha to Lakshmi

14. **Pushpam Samarpayami**:
    offer flowers to Lakshmi

15. **Ashthoththra Poojam Samarpayami**:
    offer the Holy 108 names of Lakshmi

16. **Dhoopam Aaghraapayaami**:
    offer agarbatti (incense)

17. **Deepam Darshayaami**:
    offer light

18. **Neivedyam Samarpayami** :
    offer food to Lakshmi

19. **Phalam Samarpayami**:
    offer Fruits to Lakshmi

20. **Taamboolam Samarpayami**:
    offer beetle nut and leaves

21. **Dakshinam Samarpayami**:
    offer money to Lakshmi

22. **Maha Nirajanam Samarpayami**:
    perform the main aarati

23. **Pradakshinam Samarpayami**:
    turning clockwise around Lakshmi

24. **Namaskaram Samarpayami**:
    offer prostrations

25. **Mantra Pushpam Samarpayami**:
    offer both incantations and flowers

26. **Praarthanaam Samarpayami**:
    offering prayers; list your requests

27. **Xamaapanam Samarpayami**:
    offering apologies to Lakshmi for any mistakes

note: you can use a statue, yantra or photo for the short puja.

Practice #4

Vrata

A Vrata is a promise to perform a ceremony for a certain period of time in order to generate and receive Divine grace.

For prosperity and success, the Vaibhava Lakshmi Vrat is very popular as it is quite easy to perform.

In India, this Vrata is given in small booklets in the major Indan languages. In the following pages is the essence of the the observance for this Vrata. First, the rules for observing the promise for receiving prosperity is given, then the story behind this Vrata is recounted. All the tools necessary for its performance are included

Rules for Observing the Vrata

1. Both men and women can perform the ceremony. The Vrata can be prescribed for seven or eleven or twenty-one Fridays.

2. It is recommended that the Vrata should be done at least once a year. It is possible to perform the Vrata more than once a year - the promise has to be given each time.

3. On the day of observance of the Vrat, throughout one should utter 'Jai Goddess Laxmi' or 'Jai Ma Laxmi' in the heart center as many times as possible. One should only eat once in the evening.

4. It has to be observed in one's home and so if you need to travel on that day, skip it and do it the next week. If the woman is in menses or either man or woman has a death in the family on the Friday, one should observe the Vrat the following Friday. As long as you observe the correct number of Fridays, it is permitted to skip one or more Fridays.

5. In the beginning of observing the Vrat, one should recite once the hymn or praise the Goddess Laxmi.

6. Material needed: the Shree Yantra or mystical diagram and pictures of various forms of Lakshmi. A gold or silver or a dollar coin for ornamentation.

7. One should bow down one's head to each and every incarnation of Goddess Laxmi given above. And also, while observing the Vrat one should pay homage to Shri Yantra.

8. To celebrate the completion of the Vrat one should give a copy of this book to someone else - to one, seven, eleven, twenty-one, fifty-one or hundred and one people according to one's own desire.

The Story of the Vaibhav Lakshmi Vrat

Once upon a time there was a large city devoted to sensual enjoyment. The inhabitants engaged themselves in material affairs and there was hardly any development of the virtues of devotion, benevolence, sympathy and affection. In fact, they gloried in their vices, indulging incessantly in alcohol, gambling, illegal relationships and every heinous activity imaginable.

Despite the prevailing atmosphere of vice, a few spiritually minded people lived the virtuous life like the lotus in the muddy waters of the pond. Among this small group was Sheela and her husband, Vijay. He was a humble, honest and hard working man with a good character while she was of a spiritual nature and very deovoted to the worship of the Divine Mother. Everyone praised them and they seemed like an ideal couple, but many also cast envious eyes upon them.

Due to the karmic consequences of negative actions from prevous lifes, Vijay found himself in the company of rogues who pretended to be his friends. Their influence caused Vijay to desire wealth beyond all reason and he started to speculate on all manners of gambling. To keep up with his friends, he indulged in drinking and other forms of sensual gratification. He lost all his money and then had to sell his wife's jewellery to keep going. They eventually became so poor that they could not even afford food to satisfy their hunger. All his fair-weather friends deserted him and he sank into despression.

During all this time, Sheela never lost faith or gave up and did her best to help her husband. She knew that in every life, there are cycles when unhappiness will be followed by happiness while happiness will be followed by unhappiness. With faith in this eternal truth, she maintained her spiritual practice with hope for a brighter future.

One day at noontime someone came knocking at her door. Even though she had nothing to offer anyone , instilled with the Aryan culture of welcoming guests at the door, she went to open her doors.

There stood an old woman whose face was dazzling with the glow of divine light , and from whose eyes dripped the nectar of compassion and love. Sheela immediately experienced immense peace in her heart and welcomed her by offering the only torn and tattered mat for sitting. The old lady said, "Sheela! Don't you know me?"

Sheela humbly said, "Mother, I'm delighted to see you and feel peace in the soul, as if I have been searching a long time for you, but you are a stranger !' The old lady smiled, " Did you forget me? Every Friday we would meet at the temple of the Goddess Lakshmi!"

Since they had fallen on hard times, Sheela had stopped going to the Temple out of shame, but hard as she tried, she was unable to recall having seen the old lady before. After a while, the old lady mused, "How sweet you sang the prayer of Goddess Lakshmi with the other devotees!" It's been some time since you've gone to the temple and so I've come to see how your are doing.

Sheela started to cry when she heard the old lady's kind words. The older woman patted the sobbing Sheela to console her and said, "My dear, happiness and sorrow are like the heat and shadow of the Sun. Happiness and misery come one after the other. Please have patience and tell me all about your sufferings. You will get the remedy for your pain."

Between sobs, Sheela recounted her troubles and hopes. The old lady said, 'Dear, happiness and sorrow come one after the other. It is difficult to foresee the working of karma. Everyone has to suffer the consequences of good or bad deeds. Don't worry. You and your husband have already suffered enough. Happy days are here again. You are the devotee of Goddess Lakshmi who is the incarnation of love and compassion. She is very merciful to her devotees. Hence, have patience and observe the Vrat of the Goddess and your life will be quite easy-going."

Wiping her tears away, Sheela said to the old lady, "Mother! Kindly tell me how the Vrat of Lakshmiji can be observed." The old lady responded, "The Vrat of Lakshmiji is very easy to follow. It is called the 'Vaibhava Lakshmi Vrat' (Promise giving wealth) or 'Vaibhava Lakshmi Vrat' (Promise giving Luxury). All the hopes of the person who observes the Vrat, will get fulfilled, and she or he becomes happy, wealthy and reputed."

Then she began to describe how to perform the Vrat. "The Vrat should be observed on Friday every week. One should put on clean clothes after bathing in the morning and should utter silently 'Jai Ma Lakshmi'. One should not speak evil of others during the day. Having washed hands and feet in the evening, one should sit on the wooden seat facing the east direction. Set up a big wooden seat, and then put a copper pot on the small heaps of rice arranged on a handkerchief spread on the wooden seat. Keep gold or a silver ornament or a rupee coin in a small bowl placed on the copper pot. Light the lamp-stand and the incense stick near the wooden seat."

She continued, "there are many incarnations of Goddess Lakshmi. A person observing the Vrat should devotedly look at the 'Shree Yantra or mystical diagram' and the various forms of the Goddess. Then one should sing the prayer of Lakshmi. Afterwards apply yellow or red tumeric with rice grain on the ornaments or rupee-coin. Then after adorning it with a red flower, one should wave lights keeping sweets or piece of jaggery (solid molasses) and should utter 'Jai Ma Lakshmi'. After the rituals, offer the blessed food or prasad among the members of the family. That ornament or a rupee-coin should be put in a safe place. The water kept in the copper-bowl should be poured into a pot of basil-plant [tulasi] and the rice grain should be thrown to the birds. In this way one gets his or her desires fulfilled by observing the Vrat according to the prescribed ceremony of the shastras - a man gets wealthy by Her grace; an unmarried girl gets married; the married woman maintains a happy relationship, and a childless woman gets a child."

In conclusion, the old lady said, "this Vaibhava Lakshmi Vrat should be done for eleven or twenty-one Fridays. On the last Friday, the Vrat should be celebrated by offering a coconut and sweet dish of rice. On that day the sweets should be given to seven unmarried girls or ladies while repeating…' Jai Ma Vaibhava Lakshmi' and they should each be given a book of 'Vaibhava Lakshmi Vrat'. Afterwards you should bow down your head to a photograph of Goddess Dhanlaksmi with the following prayer in your heart - 'Mother! I have observed the Vaibhava Lakhsmi Vrat. Please fulfill all our wishes! Kindly give wealth to the poor and give children to the childless woman. Let the married woman enjoy the happy state of wifehood. Let the unmarried girl fulfill her desires. Pour your grace on those who observe your Vrat and be kind to them by favoring happiness in their lives'. Then, keeping your hands above (not to touch) the flames of the lamp, apply it to your eyes."

Sheela immediately closed her eyes made her promise to the Goddess to perfrom the Vrat for twenty-one Fridays. When she opened her eyes, she was very much surprised to find that the old lady had disappeared! That old lady was no one else but Lakshmi Herself!

The very next day was Friday. After bathing, Sheela began to utter, 'Jai Ma Laksmii' with full faith in the Goddess. During the day she didn't defame any one. In the evening having washed her hands and feet, Sheela placed the wooden seat and put her nose-ornament in the small bowl placed on the copper pot, which was on the heaps of rice arranged on the handkerchief spread on the wooden seat. Sitting in the east, Sheela observed the Vrat as taught by that old lady. Then she offered some sugar to her husband. Immediately there was a great change in her husband's nature and he remembered how things were before he fell in with a bad crowd. He cried and apologized for his misbehavior. By the time she had performed the Vrat for 21 Fridays, her life had become totally blessed. Vijay had gone to work and recovered his wealth and in fact had become much wealthier. Both were in their best health, and had many good friends. Both went to the Lakshmi Temple and sang the praises of the Mother.

Having seen the pious power of the Vaibhava Laxmi Vrat, other women began to perform the Vrat according to the ceremony described by Sheela.

Oh! Goddess Dhan Lakshmi! Be merciful to all, as you had been to Sheela. Fulfill the desires of all. Bless all with peace and bliss. Jai Ma Dhan Lakshmi! Jai Ma Vaibhava Laxmi!!.

Procedure for Observing the Vrata

1. One should gaze at the "Shree Yantra " or the sacred diagram of Goddess Lakshmi , uttering Salutation. One should bow down one's head to it and then apply one's hands to one's own eyes.

2. Then one should bow down one's head to the photographs of the eight incarnations of Goddess Laxmiji, and touch with hands to one's eyes. The incarnations of Goddess Laxmiji are as follows:
* Dhan Laxmi or the incarnation of Vaibhava Laxmi
* Shri Gaja Laxmi Goddess.
* Shri Adhi Laxmi Goddess.
* Shri ViJaia Laxmi Goddess.
* Shri Aishvarya Laxmi Goddess.
* Shree Veera Laxmi Goddess.
* Shri Dhanya Laxmi Goddess.
* Shri Santan Laxmi Goddess.

3. Then one should recite the following praise of Goddess Laxmi. Apply red or yellow powder on the ornament:

Ya raktambuj vasini vilasini Chandanshu tejasvini!!
Ya rakta rudhirambera Harisakhi Ya Shree Manolhadini!
Ya ratnakarmanthanatpragatita Vishnosvaya gehini!
Sa mam patu Manorama Bhagavati Lakshmi Padmavati!!

Significance: Oh Goddess, Laxmi One who resides in the red lotus, (one) who is graceful, who has glorious rays of divine (light) luster, who is completely reddish, who is clothed in the form of blood, who is beloved to God Vishnu, Goddess Laxmi, who gives happiness to the heart, who is created by churning of the ocean, one who is the wife of God Vishnu, one who is born from the lotus, who is extremely worthy to be worshipped kindly protect me.

SHREE GODDESS DHANLAXMIJI MA
Oh! Goddesss of Dhan (Vaibhava) Lakshmi Ma! Be merciful to all
and fulfill the desires of all as you had blessed Sheela.

Mother Laxmiji, to make her happy the miracle happiness, wealth
and peace bestowing SHREE YANTRA
Before starting the Vaibhav Laxmi Vrat one must first bow their
head to Shree Yantra

SHREE GODDESS GAJA LAXMIJI

Oh! Goddess Gaja Laxmi! Be merciful to all, as you had been to Sheela. Fulfill the desires of all. Bless all with happiness.

SHRI GODDESS ADHI LAXMIJI

Oh! Supreme Mother Adhi Laxmiji! Be merciful to all, as you had favored Sheela. Fulfill the Desires of all. Bless all with happiness.

SHRI GODDESS VIJAYA LAXMIJI
Oh! Goddess of Victory, ViJaia Laxmiji! Be merciful to all, as you
had blessed Sheela. Fulfill the desires of all. Bless all with bliss.

SHRI GODDESS AAISHVARY LAXMIJI
Oh! Mother of Prosperity, Aaishvarya Laxmiji! Be merciful to all,
as you had blessed Sheela. Fulfill the desires of all.
Bless all with bliss.

SHRI GODDESS VEER LAXMIJI

Oh! Heroic Mother, Veer Laxmiji! Be merciful to all, as you
favored Sheela. Fulfill the desires of all. Bless all with happiness

SHRI DHANYA LAXMIJI

Oh! Goddess of harvest, Dhanya Laxmiji! Be merciful to all, as
you had favored Sheela. Fulfill the desires of all.
Bless all with bliss.

SHRI GODDESS SANTAN LAXMIJI
Oh! Goddess Santan Laxmiji offering children! Be merciful to all,
as you had favored Sheela Fulfill the desires of all. Bless all with
happiness

5. One should offer a sweet dish to Goddess Vaibhava Laxmi and sing a prayer.

Mahadevi Mahalakshmi Namaste Tvam Vishnu Priye
Shaktidayee Mahalakshmi Namaste Dukha bhajani "1"

Shraaiya Prapti Nimittaya Mahalakshmi Namamyaham
Patitodhdharinee Devi Namamyaham Punaha Punaha "2"

Vedanstvam Sanstuvanti Hee shastrani Cha murhumuhu
Devastvam Pranamanti Hee Laxmi Devi Namostute"3"

Namaste Mahalakshmi Namaste Bhavabhanjanee
Bhaktimukti Na Labhyte Mahadevi Tvayee Krupa Vina"4"

Sukh Saubhagyam Na Prapnoti Patra Laxmi Na Vidyate
Na Tatfalam Samapnoti Mahalakshmi Namamyaham "5"

Dehi Saubhagyamarogyam Dehi Me Paramam Sukham
Namaste Aadyashkti Tvam Namaste Bheed, Bhanjanee"6"

Viddhehi Devi Kalyanam vidhehi Paramamshriyam
Vidyavantam Yashasvantam Lakshmvantam Janam Kuru"7"

Achintya Roop-charite Sarvashatru Vinashinee
Achintya Roop-charite Sarvashatru Pradayeenee "8"

Namamyaham Mahalakshmi Namamyaham Sureshvaree
Namamyaham Jagdhdhatree Namamyaham Parameshvaree"9"

Then one should recite the following verse to obtain immediate fruits of the Vrat.

Patrabhyagvadanman Charan
Prakashshalan Bhojan!
Satseva Pitrudevarchan Vidhihi
Satyamgavam Palanam!
Dhanya Namapi Samgraho Na
Kalahaschitta Truroopa Priya!
Drashta Praha Hari Vasami Kamala
Tasmin Gruhe Nischala!

SIGNIFICANCE

I always reside there, where guests are welcomed and offered meals, where virtuous people are rendered services, where God is worshiped and other religious services is done, where truth is observed, where no misdeed is done, where cows are protected, where corn is collected to give for charity, where there is no quarrelling, where wife is contented and polite. At the remaining places, I rarely show my favor.

6. One should then wave the light and chant the aarti:

Om Jai Laxmimata, Mayya Jai Laxmimata
Tumko Nishdin Sevat, Har Vishnu Vidhata - Om

Uma Rama Brhmani, Tumhi Jagmata
Surya Chandrma Dhyavat, Narad rushi Ghata - Om

Durga Roop Niranjani, Sukh-Sampattidata
Jo Koyi Tumko Dhyata, Rudhdhi-Sidhdhi pata – Om

Tum Patal Nivasini, Tum hi Subh data
Karm-Prabhav-Prakashini, Bhav nidhiki Trata -Om

Jis Gharme Tum Raheti, Sab sadgun Aata
Sab Sambhav Hojata, Man Nahi Ghabarata - Om

Tum bin Yagna Na Hoye, Vastrana Koyee Pata
Khan-Panka Vaibhava, Sab Tumse Aata - Om

Subhgun Mandir Sunder, Kshirodadhi jata
Ratna Chaturdas Tum bin, Koyee Nahi Pata - Om

Maha Laxmijiki Aarati, Je Koyee Nar gata
Ur Anand Samata, Pap Utar jata - Om

Bolo Maha Laxmi Mataki Jai

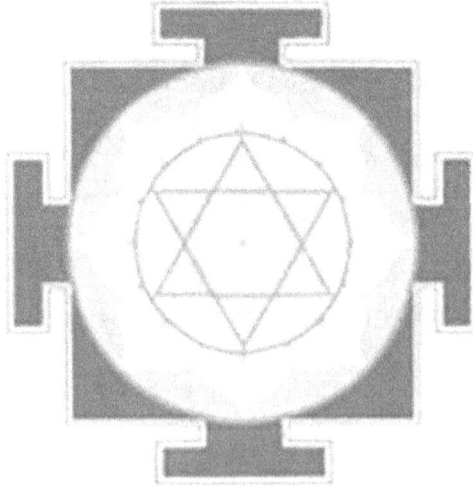

More books from Alight Publications

Breathe Like Your Life Depends On It

Author: *Rudra Shivananda*

Explore the secrets of Life-force control and expansion for self-Healing, strength and vitality. Imagine living a life protected from stress and ill-health, with wisdom and strength. This is the fruit of controlling and expanding the life-force energy called *prana*. Powerful, simple and beneficial practices which utilize the life-force in the breath, to rejuvenate the body and transform our emotional, mental and spiritual being.

[208 pages. US$18.5]

Chakra selfHealing by the power of *OM*

Author: *Rudra Shivananda*

A practical workbook on healing and spiritual evolution. Tap into the potential of the primary energy centers of the body, to eliminate depression and fatigue, relieve anxiety and stress, and calm the mind to achieve inner happiness. Learn the effective *yogic* system of tuning, balancing, color healing, rejuvenation, emotional detoxification, energization, and transcendence, with the *chakras*, in a simple, and step-by-step practice.

[140 pages. US$15.0]

Dew-Drops of the Soul

Author: *Yogiraj Gurunath*

A unique compilation of poetic gems from a contemporary Himalayan Master, expressing the essence of his inner experience, as a guide and inspiration for all spiritual seekers.

[106 pages. US$12.5]

Earth Peace through Self Peace

Author: *Yogiraj Gurunath*

A collection of spiritual talks or *satsangs*, answering the questions from sincere seekers of truth. A Master speaks to the soul through the doorway of the heart, opening the reader to the reality of the true Self, in spite of the limitations of human language.

[164 pages. US$16.5]

The Essence of Kriya Yoga

Author: *Paramhansa Yogananda*

Awaken! Arise from dreams of littleness to the realization of the vastness within you. Kriya Yoga is an instrument through which human evolution can be quickened.... This is India's unique and deathless contribution to the world's treasury of knowledge. This is a collection of the works of the most influential Yoga Master who has lived and taught in the West.

[336 pages, US$18.5]

Healing Postures of the 18 Siddhas

Author: *Rudra Shivananda*

A clear, concise and easy to follow text on the series of 18 postures widely used in Kriya Yoga. For the first time, the spiritual and mental dimensions have been revealed to supplement the physical and healing benefits of practising these postures. Fully illustrated with clear photos.

[108 pages, US$12.5]

In Light of Kriya Yoga

Author: *Rudra Shivananda*
An adept of Kriya Yoga has provided practical guidance to all those interested in expanding their awareness. What you need to know about: Self-Realization, Liberation, The Role of a Guru, Grace and Devotion, Living Joyfully, Living spiritually in a material world, Concentration and Meditation as well as other profound keys to Life.
[255 pages, US$18.5]

Practical Meditations

Author: *Paramhansa Yogananda*
Most people would like to meditate if they understood how to do so. The purpose of meditation is to know God, to connect the little joy of the soul with the vast joy of the spirit. In these three complete works of the spiritual dynamo known as Yogananada are the keys to happiness and bliss in this life.
[388 pages, US$22.95]

Surya Yoga

Author: *Rudra Shivananda*
Tap into the awesome, everpresent healing power of our life-giving Sun. Through the sincere and constant practice of the *Surya Sadhana* [solar practice], you will heal the physical body, acquire greater vitality, overcome all negativity, and also come to a greater understanding and realization of your true nature. Illustrated step-by-step instructions.
[164 pages, US$16.5]

Time and the Human Condition

Author: *Partap Singh*

Time, perspective, and our ability to understand, will reveal steps we can take to solve some of the more vexing problems of the modern world. To help us better understand ourselves and the world around us, light is shed on the nature of time, how our views of the afterlife affect our conduct in this life, how limited perspective affect education, government, and justice and how our sense of time affect our attitudes on stress and love. [220 pages, $13.5]

Wings to Freedom

Author: *Yogiraj Gurunath Siddhanath*

Mystic Revelations fom the immortal Babaji and other Himalayan Yogis, as experienced by a perfected Master, Yogiraj Gurunath Siddhanath. Follow his footsteps and experience through his words, as he walks his talk in the jungles, temples, ashrams and hidden [to the uninitiated] places of India. Enrich your life with the secret oral traditions revealed for the first time - mysteries of life, immortality and the attainment of Self-Realization. [308 pages, US$18.5]

Yoga of Purification and Transformation

Author: *Rudra Shivananda*

Attain Peace of Mind in this life and Terminate the cycle of suffering caused by the accumulation of negative karma. Learn the 5 yogic restraints or yamas which constitute the Yoga of Purification and the 5 yogic observances or niyamas which are the heart of the Yoga of Transformation. An inspiring and informative presentation of the often neglected foundation of all successful spiritual practice. Actual detailed practices are given in addition to relevant examples and parables. [220 pages, US$18.5]

For information on these or other books or to purchase them:
htttp://www.alightbooks.com